THIS BOOK

BELONGS TO

....

....

Thank you for Purchasing my book and taking the time to read it from front to back. I am always grateful when a reader chooses my work and I hope you enjoyed it!

With the vast selection available online, I am touched that you chose to be purchasing my work and take valuable time out of your life to read it. My hope is that you feel you made the right decision.

I very much would like to know what you thought of the book. Please take the time to write an honest and informative review on Amazon.com. Your experience and opinions will be of great benefit to me and those readers looking to make an informed choice.

With much thanks.

Table of Contents

SUMMARY

The Beauty and Diversity of Crochet Stitches: Crochet, a versatile and intricate craft, offers a wide range of stitches that showcase the beauty and diversity of this art form. From simple stitches to complex patterns, crochet stitches allow for endless possibilities in creating stunning and unique designs.

One of the most basic crochet stitches is the single crochet. This stitch creates a dense and sturdy fabric, making it perfect for items like blankets or scarves. It involves inserting the hook into the previous stitch, yarn over, and pulling through both loops on the hook. The single crochet stitch can be easily mastered by beginners and serves as a foundation for more advanced stitches.

Moving on to more intricate stitches, the double crochet stitch adds height and texture to crochet projects. This stitch involves yarn over, inserting the hook into the previous stitch, yarn over again, and pulling through the first two loops on the hook. This process is repeated until only one loop remains on the hook. The double crochet stitch is commonly used in creating lacy patterns and openwork designs.

For those looking to add even more complexity to their crochet projects, the treble crochet stitch is a great choice. This stitch is taller than the double crochet and creates a more open and airy fabric. To execute the treble crochet stitch, yarn over twice, insert the hook into the previous stitch, yarn over, and pull through the first two loops on the hook. Repeat this process until only one loop remains on the hook. The treble crochet stitch is often used in creating intricate lace patterns and delicate shawls.

Beyond these basic stitches, there are countless variations and combinations that can be explored. The shell stitch, for example, is created by working multiple stitches into the same stitch or space, resulting in a scalloped or shell-like appearance. This stitch is commonly used in creating decorative borders or adding texture to blankets and garments.

Another popular stitch is the granny square, which is made up of clusters of double crochet stitches worked in the round. This versatile stitch can be used to create blankets, scarves, or even entire garments. The granny square is often associated with traditional crochet designs and is a favorite among crocheters for its simplicity and versatility.

In addition to these individual stitches, crochet patterns often incorporate a combination of stitches to create intricate and visually stunning designs. From intricate cables to delicate lacework, crochet stitches can be combined in endless ways to achieve unique and personalized creations.

The beauty and diversity of crochet stitches are not limited to their appearance alone. Crocheting offers a therapeutic and

Embarking on a Journey of Stitches, Textures, and Techniques of Crochet Stitches:

Crochet, a versatile and creative craft, offers a world of possibilities for those who embark on a journey of stitches, textures, and techniques. Whether you are a beginner or an experienced crocheter, there is always something new to learn and explore in the realm of crochet stitches.

One of the most exciting aspects of crochet is the vast array of stitches available to create unique and intricate designs. From basic stitches like single crochet and double crochet to more complex stitches like the popcorn stitch and the crocodile stitch, each stitch adds its own texture and character to your crochet projects. By mastering different stitches, you can create beautiful patterns, textures, and even three-dimensional effects in your work.

Textures play a crucial role in crochet, adding depth and visual interest to your projects. By combining different stitches and techniques, you can create a variety of textures, from smooth and sleek to bumpy and chunky. The choice of yarn also plays a significant role in determining the texture of your crochet work. Experimenting with different yarn weights and fibers can lead to stunning results, allowing you to create soft and cozy blankets, delicate lacework, or sturdy and durable garments.

Techniques in crochet encompass a wide range of skills and methods that can elevate your projects to new heights. From colorwork and tapestry crochet to Tunisian crochet and filet crochet, each technique offers its own unique challenges and rewards. Learning these techniques opens up a world of possibilities, allowing you to create intricate patterns, beautiful motifs, and even pictures in your crochet work.

Embarking on a journey of stitches, textures, and techniques in crochet is not only a creative endeavor but also a therapeutic and relaxing activity. The repetitive nature of crochet stitches can be soothing and calming, providing a sense of mindfulness and focus. Many crocheters find solace in the rhythmic motion of their hooks and yarn, allowing them to unwind and de-stress from the demands of everyday life.

Furthermore, crochet is a craft that can be enjoyed by people of all ages and skill levels. Whether you are a child learning the basics or an adult looking to expand your creative horizons, crochet offers a welcoming and inclusive community. Online forums, social media groups, and local crochet clubs provide a platform for crocheters to connect, share ideas, and inspire one another.

What to Expect from This Guide of Crochet Stitches: In this comprehensive guide, you can expect to learn everything you need to know about crochet stitches. Whether you are a beginner looking to start your crochet journey or an experienced crocheter wanting to expand your stitch repertoire, this guide has got you covered.

First and foremost, we will provide you with a clear and concise explanation of the basic crochet stitches. From the foundational chain stitch to the versatile single, double, and treble crochet stitches, we will break down each stitch step-by-step, ensuring that you understand the technique and can execute it with confidence.

But we won't stop there. This guide will also introduce you to a wide range of advanced crochet stitches that will take your projects to the next level. You will learn about intricate stitches such as the popcorn stitch, shell stitch, and cable stitch, among many others. With detailed instructions and accompanying visuals, you will be able to create stunning textures and patterns in your crochet work.

In addition to learning individual stitches, we will also explore various stitch combinations and techniques. You will discover how to create beautiful stitch patterns by combining different stitches, allowing you to add depth and complexity to your projects. We will also delve into techniques such as colorwork, tapestry crochet, and filet crochet, enabling you to incorporate unique designs and motifs into your creations.

Furthermore, this guide will provide you with tips and tricks to improve your crochet skills. We will discuss common mistakes to avoid, offer guidance on tension control, and share techniques for achieving clean and even stitches. Additionally, we will provide suggestions for selecting the right yarn and hook size for your projects, ensuring that you achieve the desired results.

To help you put your newfound knowledge into practice, we will include a variety of crochet patterns that showcase different stitches and techniques. These patterns will range from simple and quick projects, perfect for beginners, to more complex and intricate designs for those seeking a challenge. Each pattern will come with detailed instructions and helpful tips, allowing you to create beautiful and professional-looking crochet items.

Whether you aspire to crochet cozy blankets, stylish garments, or adorable amigurumi toys, this guide will equip you with the skills and knowledge to bring your creative visions to life. With its comprehensive coverage of crochet stitches, techniques, and patterns, this guide is your ultimate resource for all things crochet. So grab your yarn and hook, and get ready to embark on a crochet journey filled with endless possibilities.

Basic Stitches and Techniques Every Crocheter Should Know: Crocheting is a popular and versatile craft that allows you to create beautiful and functional items using just a hook and yarn. Whether you're a beginner or an experienced crocheter, there are certain basic stitches and techniques that are essential to know in order to successfully complete various crochet projects.

One of the most fundamental stitches in crochet is the chain stitch. This stitch forms the foundation of most crochet projects and is used to create a starting row or to add length to a project. To create a chain stitch, you simply yarn over and pull the yarn through the loop on your hook, repeating this process until you have the desired number of chains.

Another important stitch is the single crochet. This stitch is used to create a tight and dense fabric and is often used in amigurumi projects or to create solid pieces such as blankets or scarves. To work a single crochet, you insert your hook into the next stitch, yarn over, and pull the yarn through the stitch. Then, yarn over again and pull through both loops on your hook.

The double crochet stitch is another commonly used stitch in crochet. It creates a taller and more open fabric compared to the single crochet. To work a double crochet, you yarn over, insert your hook into the next stitch, yarn over again, and pull the yarn through the stitch. Then, yarn over once more and pull through the first two loops on your hook, yarn over again and pull through the remaining two loops.

Once you have mastered these basic stitches, you can move on to more advanced techniques such as increasing and decreasing stitches. Increasing stitches allows you to add width or shape to your project, while decreasing stitches helps you create shaping or tapering. These techniques are often used in garment making or when creating intricate patterns.

In addition to stitches, there are also various techniques that can enhance your crochet projects. One such technique is color changing, which allows you to create beautiful patterns and designs by switching yarn colors. This technique is commonly used in projects such as blankets, scarves, or garments.

Another important technique is joining pieces together. This is often done when creating larger projects that require multiple pieces to be sewn or crocheted together. There are several methods for joining, including slip stitching, whip stitching, or crocheting the pieces together.

Understanding Yarn Weights, Hooks, and Materials of Crochet Stitches: When it comes to crochet, understanding yarn weights, hooks, and materials is essential for creating beautiful and well-finished projects. Yarn weight refers to the thickness of the yarn, which can greatly impact the final look and feel of your crochet work. Hooks, on the other hand, determine the size of the stitches and play a crucial role in achieving the desired tension and gauge. Lastly, the choice of materials, such as natural fibers or synthetic blends, can affect the drape, durability, and overall quality of your crochet pieces.

Yarn weight is typically categorized into several standardized categories, ranging from lace weight to super bulky. Each weight has its own recommended hook size and gauge, which helps ensure that your stitches are consistent and your finished project turns out as intended. Lace weight yarn is the thinnest and requires a small hook size, resulting in delicate and intricate designs. On the other end of the spectrum, super bulky yarn is thick and requires a larger hook size, resulting in quick and chunky projects.

Hooks come in various sizes and materials, such as aluminum, plastic, or wood. The size of the hook determines the size of the stitches, with smaller hooks creating tighter stitches and larger hooks creating looser stitches. It's important to match the hook size to the recommended size for the yarn weight you are using to achieve the correct tension and gauge. Additionally, the material of the hook can affect the grip and comfort while crocheting, so it's worth experimenting with different materials to find the one that suits you best.

When it comes to materials, the choice between natural fibers and synthetic blends can greatly impact the final outcome of your crochet project. Natural fibers, such as cotton, wool, or silk, offer breathability, softness, and a natural drape. They are often preferred for garments and accessories that require warmth or a luxurious feel. Synthetic blends, on the other hand, offer durability, affordability, and a wide range of colors and textures. They are often used for projects that require easy care or vibrant colors.

Understanding yarn weights, hooks, and materials is crucial for achieving the desired results in your crochet projects. By selecting the appropriate yarn weight, matching it with the right hook size, and choosing the ideal material, you can create stunning and well-finished crochet pieces that showcase your skills and creativity. So, take the time to familiarize yourself with these aspects of crochet and enjoy the endless possibilities they offer in your crafting journey.

Deciphering Patterns, Symbols, and Abbreviations of Crochet Stitches: Deciphering Patterns, Symbols, and Abbreviations of Crochet Stitches is a comprehensive guide that aims to provide a detailed understanding of the various patterns, symbols, and abbreviations used in the world of crochet.

Crochet is a popular craft that involves creating fabric by interlocking loops of yarn using a crochet hook. It is a versatile and creative hobby that allows individuals to create a wide range of items, from clothing and accessories to home decor and toys. However, one of the challenges that beginners often face is deciphering the patterns, symbols, and abbreviations that are commonly used in crochet instructions.

This guide is designed to address this challenge by breaking down the different elements of crochet patterns and providing clear explanations and examples. It starts by introducing the basic stitches and techniques used in crochet, ensuring that readers have a solid foundation before delving into more complex patterns.

The guide then moves on to explain the various symbols and abbreviations that are commonly used in crochet patterns. These symbols and abbreviations serve as a shorthand way of conveying instructions, allowing crocheters to quickly understand and follow a pattern. However, for beginners, these symbols and abbreviations can be confusing and overwhelming. This guide aims to demystify them by providing clear explanations and visual representations.

In addition to explaining the symbols and abbreviations, the guide also provides examples of how they are used in different patterns. This allows readers to see how the symbols and abbreviations translate into actual stitches and patterns, making it easier for them to understand and follow crochet instructions.

Furthermore, the guide includes tips and tricks for deciphering patterns, symbols, and abbreviations. It offers strategies for breaking down complex patterns into manageable steps, as well as techniques for troubleshooting common issues that may arise during the crochet process.

Overall, Deciphering Patterns, Symbols, and Abbreviations of Crochet Stitches is a valuable resource for both beginners and experienced crocheters. It provides a comprehensive understanding of the different elements of crochet patterns, ensuring that readers can confidently tackle any project they choose. With its clear explanations, visual representations, and helpful tips, this guide is a must-have for anyone looking to enhance their crochet skills and expand their repertoire of stitches and patterns.

Creating Your First Simple Project of Crochet Stitches:

Crochet is a versatile and enjoyable craft that allows you to create beautiful and functional items using just a hook and some yarn. If you're new to crochet and looking to start your first project, this guide will walk you through the process of creating a simple yet stunning piece using basic crochet stitches.

Before you begin, gather your materials. You'll need a crochet hook, which comes in various sizes, and a ball of yarn in the color of your choice. It's recommended to start with a medium-weight yarn and a corresponding hook size, such as a size H/8 (5mm) hook. Additionally, you may want to have a pair of scissors and a yarn needle on hand for finishing touches.

Once you have your materials ready, it's time to choose a project. For beginners, a great option is to create a simple scarf or a dishcloth. These projects are relatively quick to complete and allow you to practice the basic crochet stitches.

To start, make a slipknot by creating a loop with the yarn and pulling the end through. Insert your crochet hook into the loop and tighten it. This slipknot will serve as the foundation for your project.

Next, you'll need to create a foundation chain. This is a series of chain stitches that will determine the width of your project. To make a chain stitch, yarn over (wrap the yarn around the hook from back to front) and pull it through the loop on your hook. Repeat this process until you have the desired number of chain stitches. For a scarf, aim for around 30-40 chain stitches, while a dishcloth may require fewer.

Once you have your foundation chain, it's time to move on to the main stitches. The most basic stitch in crochet is the single crochet (sc). To make a single crochet stitch, insert your hook into the second chain from the hook, yarn over, and pull the yarn through the chain stitch. You should now have two loops on your hook. Yarn over again and pull through both loops. Congratulations, you've just completed your first single crochet stitch!

Continue making single crochet stitches across the row, inserting your hook into the next chain stitch, yarn over, pull through, yarn over, and pull through both loops. Repeat this process until you reach the end of the row. This will create the foundation row for your project.

To start the next row, turn your work and make a chain

An Introduction to Textured Stitches in Crochet:

Exploring the World of Intricate Patterns and Unique Textures

Crochet, a beloved craft that has been passed down through generations, offers endless possibilities for creativity and self-expression. While the basic stitches like single crochet and double crochet are essential for creating beautiful projects, there is a whole world of textured stitches waiting to be discovered. These stitches add depth, dimension, and visual interest to your crochet work, elevating it from ordinary to extraordinary.

Textured stitches in crochet are created by combining various combinations of basic stitches, such as front post double crochet, back post double crochet, popcorn stitch, and shell stitch, among others. These stitches create raised or recessed areas on the fabric, resulting in a tactile and visually appealing texture. They can be used to mimic the look of cables, ribbing, lace, or even create unique patterns that are exclusive to crochet.

One of the most popular textured stitches in crochet is the bobble stitch. This stitch creates small, rounded clusters of stitches that pop out from the fabric, resembling tiny bobbles. It adds a playful and whimsical touch to any project, making it perfect for baby blankets, scarves, or even hats. The bobble stitch can be easily mastered with a little practice and adds a delightful texture that is sure to impress.

Another fascinating textured stitch is the crocodile stitch. This stitch creates a scale-like pattern that resembles the skin of a crocodile. It is perfect for creating eye-catching accessories like bags, shawls, or even gloves. The crocodile stitch may seem complex at first, but with clear instructions and a bit of patience, you'll be able to create stunning pieces that are sure to turn heads.

If you're looking for a stitch that adds elegance and sophistication to your crochet work, the cable stitch is a perfect choice. This stitch creates interlocking cables that mimic the look of knitted cables. It is ideal for creating cozy sweaters, blankets, or even socks. While the cable stitch may require a bit more concentration and practice, the end result is well worth the effort, as it adds a touch of timeless beauty to your projects.

Exploring the world of textured stitches in crochet opens up a whole new realm of possibilities for your creativity. By incorporating these stitches into your projects, you can transform simple patterns into intricate works of art.

Learning the Bobble, Popcorn, and Puff Stitches in Crochet: Crochet is a popular craft that involves creating fabric by interlocking loops of yarn using a crochet hook. There are numerous stitches and techniques that can be learned and mastered in crochet, each adding its own unique texture and design to the finished project. In this particular case, we will focus on three stitches: the Bobble, Popcorn, and Puff stitches.

The Bobble stitch is a fun and decorative stitch that adds a three-dimensional texture to your crochet work. It is created by working multiple double crochet stitches into the same stitch or space, and then finishing them all together. This creates a cluster of stitches that pop out from the fabric, resembling small bobbles. The Bobble stitch can be used to create interesting patterns and designs, and it is often used in projects such as blankets, scarves, and hats.

The Popcorn stitch is another popular stitch that creates a raised texture on your crochet fabric. It is similar to the Bobble stitch, but instead of working multiple double crochet stitches into the same stitch or space, you work multiple double crochet stitches into the same stitch and then remove the hook from the loop. This creates a small popcorn shape that stands out from the fabric. The Popcorn stitch can be used to create decorative elements in your crochet work, such as flowers or polka dots, and it adds a playful and whimsical touch to any project.

The Puff stitch is a versatile stitch that can be used to create a variety of textures and designs. It is created by working multiple yarn overs and then pulling through all the loops on the hook. This creates a cluster of stitches that puff out from the fabric, giving it a soft and fluffy appearance. The Puff stitch can be used to create patterns, such as shells or waves, and it adds a cozy and warm feel to your crochet projects.

Learning these stitches may seem intimidating at first, but with practice and patience, you will soon become comfortable with them. There are numerous tutorials and resources available online that provide step-by-step instructions and visual demonstrations on how to work these stitches. It is recommended to start with small practice swatches before incorporating these stitches into larger projects, as this will help you become more familiar with the techniques and allow you to perfect your tension and stitch consistency.

In conclusion, learning the Bobble, Popcorn, and Puff stitches in crochet opens up a world of possibilities for creating unique and textured fabric.

Cable, Twist, and Ripple Stitches in Crochet: Cable, twist, and ripple stitches are popular techniques used in crochet to create unique and visually appealing patterns. These stitches add texture and dimension to your crochet projects, making them stand out from the crowd.

The cable stitch is a technique that mimics the look of a cable knit in knitting. It involves crossing stitches over each other to create a twisted effect. This stitch is achieved by skipping a certain number of stitches, working a set of stitches in the skipped stitches, and then working the skipped stitches over the set of stitches. This creates the appearance of a twisted cable running through your crochet fabric. Cable stitches can be used to create intricate designs, such as braids or Celtic knots, and are often used in projects like scarves, hats, and blankets.

The twist stitch is another technique that adds a twist or spiral effect to your crochet work. This stitch is achieved by working a series of stitches in the same stitch or space, and then twisting the stitches around each other. This creates a spiral-like pattern that adds visual interest to your crochet fabric. Twist stitches can be used to create a variety of designs, from simple spirals to more complex motifs. They are often used in projects like shawls, cowls, and bags.

The ripple stitch is a popular technique used to create waves or ripples in your crochet fabric. This stitch is achieved by working a series of increases and decreases in a specific pattern. The increases create the peaks of the waves, while the decreases create the valleys. This creates a ripple effect that adds movement and texture to your crochet work. Ripple stitches can be used to create a variety of designs, from subtle waves to bold zigzags. They are often used in projects like blankets, scarves, and baby items.

When working with cable, twist, and ripple stitches, it is important to pay attention to your tension and stitch count. These stitches often require precise stitch placement and tension to achieve the desired effect. It is also helpful to use stitch markers or a row counter to keep track of your pattern repeats, especially when working on larger projects.

In conclusion, cable, twist, and ripple stitches are versatile techniques that can elevate your crochet projects to the next level. Whether you want to create intricate cables, spiraling twists, or flowing ripples, these stitches offer endless possibilities for adding texture and visual interest to your crochet fabric. So grab your crochet hook and yarn, and start experimenting with these stitches to create stunning and unique crochet creations.

Tips for Neat Finishing and Joining of Crochet Stitches:

When it comes to crochet, achieving a neat and professional finish is essential for creating beautiful and polished projects. The finishing and joining of crochet stitches play a crucial role in determining the overall appearance and durability of your work. To help you achieve a clean and seamless finish, here are some tips to keep in mind.

1. Weave in Ends: One of the most important steps in finishing your crochet project is weaving in the loose ends. Instead of leaving them hanging, take the time to neatly weave them into the stitches using a yarn needle. This not only ensures a tidy appearance but also prevents the ends from unraveling over time.

2. Invisible Join: When joining rounds or rows, using an invisible join technique can create a seamless and nearly invisible connection. To achieve this, slip stitch into the first stitch of the round or row, then pull the yarn through the loop on your hook and cut it, leaving a tail. Thread the tail through a yarn needle and insert it under both loops of the next stitch, skipping the slip stitch. This creates a smooth and seamless join.

3. Blocking: Blocking is a technique used to shape and smooth out your crochet project. It involves wetting or steaming the finished piece and then pinning it into the desired shape. Blocking helps to even out stitches, open up lacework, and give your project a more professional look. It is especially useful for items like shawls, blankets, and garments.

4. Invisible Decreases: When working on projects that require decreasing stitches, using an invisible decrease technique can help maintain a clean and seamless appearance. Instead of using a regular single crochet decrease, insert your hook under the front loop of the first stitch, then under the front loop of the next stitch, yarn over, and pull through both loops. This creates a decrease that is nearly invisible and blends in with the surrounding stitches.

5. Edging: Adding a neat and well-executed edging can elevate the overall look of your crochet project. Whether it's a simple single crochet border or a more intricate lace edging, taking the time to carefully work the stitches and maintain consistent tension will result in a polished finish. Edging also helps to stabilize the edges of your project and prevent them from curling.

Caring for and Maintaining Crochet Items: Caring for and maintaining crochet items is essential to ensure their longevity and keep them looking their best. Crochet items, whether it be clothing, accessories, or home decor, require special attention and care to preserve their delicate nature and intricate designs.

First and foremost, it is important to handle crochet items with care. Avoid pulling or tugging on the stitches, as this can cause them to unravel or stretch out of shape. Instead, gently handle the item by supporting it from underneath or by holding it by the edges. This will help maintain the integrity of the stitches and prevent any unnecessary damage.

When it comes to cleaning crochet items, it is best to follow the care instructions provided by the maker or designer. Some crochet items may be machine washable, while others may require hand washing. If machine washing is recommended, it is important to place the item in a mesh laundry bag or pillowcase to protect it from getting tangled or snagged on other items in the wash. Additionally, using a gentle cycle and cold water will help prevent any shrinking or distortion of the crochet stitches.

For hand washing crochet items, fill a basin or sink with lukewarm water and add a mild detergent specifically designed for delicate fabrics. Gently agitate the water to create suds, and then submerge the crochet item, making sure it is fully saturated. Allow the item to soak for a few minutes, and then gently squeeze out any excess water. Avoid wringing or twisting the item, as this can cause it to lose its shape. Rinse the item thoroughly with clean water, ensuring all soap residue is removed. To dry, lay the item flat on a clean towel, shaping it back into its original form. Avoid hanging crochet items to dry, as this can cause them to stretch out of shape.

In addition to regular cleaning, it is important to store crochet items properly to prevent any damage. Avoid folding or creasing the item, as this can create permanent lines or wrinkles. Instead, roll the item loosely and store it in a clean, dry place, such as a drawer or closet. If possible, place the item in a breathable fabric bag or pillowcase to protect it from dust and dirt.

To maintain the shape and structure of crochet items, it is recommended to use blocking techniques. Blocking involves wetting the crochet item and then shaping it to the desired dimensions. This can be done by pinning the item to a blocking board or by using blocking wires.

Continuous Learning and Advanced Techniques of Crochet Stitches:
Continuous learning and advanced techniques of crochet stitches are essential for any crochet enthusiast who wants to take their skills to the next level. By constantly expanding their knowledge and exploring new techniques, crocheters can create more intricate and complex designs, pushing the boundaries of what can be achieved with this versatile craft.

One of the key benefits of continuous learning in crochet is the ability to master a wide range of stitches. While beginners may start with basic stitches like single crochet and double crochet, advanced crocheters can delve into more intricate stitches such as the shell stitch, popcorn stitch, or cable stitch. These advanced stitches add texture, depth, and visual interest to crochet projects, elevating them from simple to stunning.

Moreover, continuous learning allows crocheters to explore different crochet techniques. For example, tapestry crochet involves working with multiple colors to create intricate patterns and designs. Tunisian crochet, also known as afghan stitch, combines elements of crochet and knitting to produce a unique fabric with a distinct texture. By learning and practicing these techniques, crocheters can expand their repertoire and create truly one-of-a-kind pieces.

In addition to expanding their stitch repertoire, continuous learning also enables crocheters to stay up-to-date with the latest trends and innovations in the crochet world. The crochet community is constantly evolving, with new patterns, techniques, and tools being introduced regularly. By staying informed and actively seeking out new information, crocheters can ensure that their work remains fresh and relevant.

Continuous learning in crochet can take many forms. It can involve attending workshops and classes, either in person or online, where experienced instructors share their knowledge and expertise. It can also involve reading books and magazines dedicated to crochet, joining crochet groups or forums to connect with fellow enthusiasts, or even watching video tutorials on platforms like YouTube.

Furthermore, continuous learning in crochet is not just about acquiring new skills and techniques, but also about honing existing ones. By practicing regularly and challenging themselves with more complex projects, crocheters can refine their skills and improve their overall craftsmanship. This dedication to continuous improvement is what sets apart a skilled crocheter from a novice.

In conclusion, continuous learning and advanced techniques of crochet stitches are crucial for crocheters who want to take their craft to new heights. By expanding their stitch repertoire, exploring different techniques, staying informed about the latest trends, and honing their skills, crocheters can create truly remarkable and unique pieces that showcase their creativity and passion for this timeless craft.

Introduction

Crocheting is a fantastic art, and you can design lots of patterns with crochet after learning its simple and modern stitches. Your practice will help you to design all simple to complicated patterns. Initially, it can be problematic to learn the stitches and techniques of crochet, but with the passage of time and practice, you can be a master in this art. The followings are some tips that can make the crocheting easy for beginners and finally, you will be able to do it while watching TV, in the car and cooking food.

Keep your Fingers and Hands Relaxed

The non-stop crocheting of 45 minutes is enough to make you tired; therefore, you should break your routine and give some time to your hand for relaxation. The stress relieving gloves will help you to get rid of pain, and you will be able to start a new session. The continuous routine can make you bore; hence, you should break the stretch of your hands and fingers to avoid cramping.

Sit in a Relaxed Posture

As you start to crochet, you have to sit in a comfortable position because an uncomfortable posture can be the reason of a backache and tiredness. There is no need to keep your head down for a longer period because this posture is not good for your backbone and shoulder. Start your work in moderation and watch for the posture while you are sitting to crochet.

Check the Tension of Yarn

The position of the yarn in your hands and tension in it matters a lot because you need to pull each loop and hold the other end tightly in your left hand. The tight and loose yarn matters a lot in your left and right hand. You should work consistently to make each row. The stitches should be super tight, and it will be based on your control on yarn. The right number of stitches will help you to design a perfect pattern.

Slowly Work on Your Patterns

The haste always makes waste; therefore, you should start slowly, but consistently to win the race. There is no need to start various projects at a time because it will ruin all your efforts. You should focus on one pattern at a time before starting another.

Fake Sticks are Good to Practice

To become a master, you need a lot of practice because you may mess up patterns in the end. If you miss even a single loop, it will make a massive hole in your pattern. You may feel aching in your hands while holding loops for a long time, but you can fake the practice to reduce tiredness. You can add a border at the start to cover up the pattern and then start working on it. Initially, the use of chunky yarn can make your work easy because it can hide lots of mistakes. You may mess up the pattern in your first attempt, but don't be disheartened because you will improve it in the next attempt.

Selection of Yarn to Crochet

The thickness of the yarn can be based on the kind of pattern, such as if you are making a blanket or thick knit cloth, then you have to use finest yarn. The chunky yarn is used to make shawls and blankets. You should check the colors, price, and quality of yarn by its pattern.

The yarn is the most important factor of crocheting because the selection of yarn can make a clear difference in the end results of the design. The yarn can be made of wool, acrylic, and cotton, but you have to consider the thickness and weight of the thread. The natural yarn may be based on cashmere, cotton, angora, silk, mohair or wool. Using the blend of natural and synthetic yarns will be good. Consider the thickness of your yarn and check the number of strands that are twisted together to make the yarn.

Selection of Crocheting Hook

A crochet hook is the most important tool with a slender handle and hook at one or both ends. You need to pull the yarn through the loops to create the crochet stitches. The crochet hooks are made of steel, plastic, Tunisian, aluminum and bamboo. The size of the crochet hook may base on the material and brand. The sizes may vary from the 0.6 mm thick hooks to 3 mm thickness. If you are going to work on larger and large patterns, such as blankets and shawls, then it will be good to use heavy hooks. The lightweight hooks are good for smaller patterns.

Chapter 1 – Tutorial for Crocodile Stitch, Picot Stitch and Waffle Stitch

Crocodile stitch is really beautiful and this stitch can turn the shapes of your projects. By adding these stitches to your project, you can give a look of art piece to your work. There will be different layers to give a unique flare to your project. You can use these stitches in different things from simple scarves to bags. Learn this stitch:

Stitch 01: Crocodile Stitch

If you want to start your crocodile stitch project, start with one slip knot, similar to all other projects, and chain 5 (make five chains) and make one chain extra. Usually, your project will determine the actual number of crochet chains. Before starting crocodile stitch, you should remember that this stitch will not work on the upper (top) layer, but work well on posts and the base of the project. If you are learning it for the first time, you should have patience and practice them slowly:

Chain multiples of five + one.

Flip and, start working into back loops, double crochet in the second chain from a crochet hook. Chain 1, *skip two chains, two double crochet into following stitch*. Replicate from * to* crosswise row.

Flip, single crochet at the base of chain. Working all the way on the back of initial post (only first one instead of both posts), five double crochet around the similar post. Now, your stitches will heap on the top of one another (each other). See in the image.

Revolve your crochet work to move back up to the opposite side and to conclude scale - working all the way around the similar singular post, front post stitch from the bottommost of your stitch up toward the top (upper part) and now work in five double crochet. The one scale is successfully completed.

Single crochet into the upper/top of the 2nd post (it will be after the only one that you have been working) to carefully hold everything to its place and continue working crosswise the row.

After completing your scales rows, you have to set up a new foundation row formerly you start your subsequent scales set: chain one at the finishing point of this scale row and flip, single crochet into the foundation of the chain. Single crochet into the center of this scale and two double crochet in the top chain between scales. Carry one crosswise row.

Once you finish and reach till the end of this row, chain 1, flip and work crosswise and make scales.

Stitch 02: Picot Stitch

This stitch is used to make edging and you can add it on the finished garment. There are numerous patterns that use combination of stitches. You can make beautiful afghan or square patterns. It will be simple to practice this stitch with the help of given tutorial:

Small PICOT Stitch:

You have to start working along the boundary of finished items. (You can make one length of the picot boundary/edge to add to your ready to wear items. You can start with one chain or one strip of sc (single crochet) or dc (double crochet)

Work Single crochet (SC) in initial stitch.

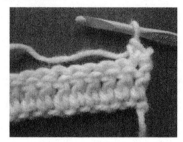

Now, Chain 3, SC (single crochet) in the subsequent stitch.

Work single crochet (SC) in the subsequent three stitches. Now, Chain 3, SC in the subsequent stitch. (The Picot is formed).

Replicate the 4th step crosswise the row.

Medium PICOT Stitch:

Replicate the instruction of small picot, but you have to chain five as an alternative of chain three.

If you want to make flared edge with picot (similar to the image), you have to work the sequence of SC (single crochet) and chain five and then single crochet again in the similar stitch.

It will help you to slightly flare out the pattern and it may become useful for the base of your tank tops, sleeves, hats and skirts.

Bauble Ended PICOT Stitch:

You have to follow all the instructions of small picot, but you have to make chain seven as a replacement of chain three.

Now Slip stitch (sl st) in the sixth stitch from your crochet hook.

SI st in the final stitch of the crochet chain. SC in the subsequent three stitches.

Replicate 1,2&3 steps crosswise the row.

Picot Stitch

The picot is a little round-shaped crochet stitch that can give a decorative edge to your work. The picots are used to fill an empty space in a web design. These are particularly made with thread, but you can try them with your yarn:

You need to create three chain stitches from the particular point in the row where you want to add a picot stitch.

Insert the hook in the 3rd chain to create the chain stitch for the preceding step.

Yarn through and design the yarn over the stitch and over the loop on the hook. You will get one complete picot stitch.

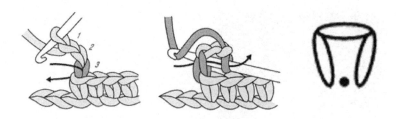

Stitch 03: Waffle Stitch

You will work on this stitch with 5.5 mm crochet hook and 4 ply worsted yarn. You will also need tapestry needle.

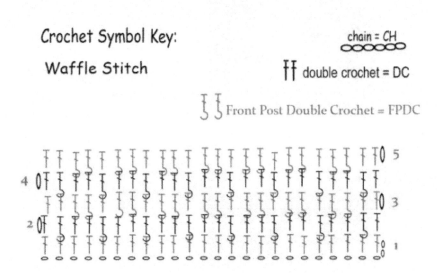

Abbreviations

DC - Double Crochet

HDC - Half Double Crochet

CH - Chain

SL ST - Slip Stitch

FPDC - Front Post Double Crochet

Instructions for Stitches:

Version for Right Hand - FPDC – Start by wrapping the YO your crochet hook, now insert the crochet hook toward the right side of your post, among the stitches, all the way around the rear and by the conflicting side among the crochet stitches toward the left side of your post. Now, wrap the YO, draw it through, finish the dc (double) crochet.

Version for Left Hand - FPDC - YO on your crochet hook, now insert the crochet hook toward the leftward of this post, among the stitches, nearby the back and by the conflicting side among the stitches toward the right area of this post. Now YO, draw it through, conclude the dc (double crochet).

Important Note: You have to work on this stitch pattern with different crochet hooks and yarn.

Now Multiple: 03

Directions:

Chain 26

Row 1: Omit two chains, work 1 DOUBLE CROCHET in every chain crosswise. (24 DOUBLE CROCHET total) flip.

Row 2: Work a chain, this will not count as a stitch, Work a double crochet in the initial stitch, *FRONT-POST-DOUBLE CROCHET around the subsequent stitch. Work a DOUBLE CROCHET in every of the subsequent two stitches. Continue crosswise from *; the last two stitches will be an FRONT-POST-DOUBLE CROCHET and a DOUBLE CROCHET, flip.

Row 3: Work a chain, this is the step up, this will not count as a stitch, Work a double crochet in the first stitch, work a DOUBLE CROCHET in the subsequent stitch, work an FRONT-POST-DOUBLE CROCHET around every of the subsequent 2 stitches. *Work a DOUBLE CROCHET in the subsequent stitch, work an FRONT-POST-DOUBLE CROCHET around the subsequent 2 stitches. Continue crosswise from *; the last two stitches will be a DOUBLE CROCHET in every stitch, flip.

Row 4: Work a chain, this is the step up, this will not count as a stitch, Work a double crochet in the initial stitch, *Work an FRONT-POST-DOUBLE CROCHET in the subsequent stitch. Work a DOUBLE CROCHET in every of the subsequent two stitches, Continue crosswise from *, the last two stitches will be an FRONT-POST-DOUBLE CROCHET and DOUBLE CROCHET in every stitch, flip.

Row 5: Work a chain, this is the step up, this will not count as a stitch, Work a double crochet in the initial stitch, *Work an FRONT-POST-DOUBLE CROCHET in every of the subsequent two stitches. Work a DOUBLE CROCHET in the subsequent stitch, Continue crosswise from *, the last two stitches will be a DOUBLE CROCHET in every stitch, flip.

Replicate Rows 2,3,4 and5.

Chapter 2 – Learn Chinese Puzzle Stitch and Cable Stitch

There are some beautiful stitches that will help you to make your own crochet patterns. You should try these stitches.

Stitch 04: Chinese Puzzle Stitch

5.5 mm crochet hook

Multiple of Stitch: CH (chain) one multiple of seven stitches and add one additional four stitches for the initial chain.

Final Dimensions: 8x8 inches block

Abbreviations:

ch – chain

R – row

RS – right side

st – stitch

sts – stitches

dc – double crochet

dc5tog – double crochet 5 together

FPdc2tog – front post double crochet 2 together

FPdc5tog – front post double crochet 5 together

decrease – is used to refer to any of the dc5tog, FPdc2tog or FPdc5tog sts

Learn Special Stitches:

dc5tog: (double-crochet-five-stitches-together) – For this stitch, you have to make five stitches – * YO (yarn over) the crochet hook, inset your crochet hook into subsequent stitch; YO the hook and draw up one loop; YO the crochet hook and draw the crochet hook through two loops on the crochet hook* reiterate from *to* four more times; YO the crochet hook and pull through six loops on your crochet hook.

FPdc2tog (front-post-double-crochet-2-together) – For this stitch, you have to make two stitches – * YO the crochet hook, inset the crochet hook from front-to-back, to front, around this post of subsequent double crochet, YO the crochet hook and draw up one loop, YO the crochet hook and pull through two loops on your crochet hook * replicate from *to* one time again; YO the crochet hook and drag through all three residual loops on your crochet hook

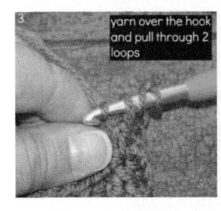

FPdc5tog (front-post-double-crochet-5-together): For this stitch, you have to make more than five stitches – * YO your crochet hook, and insert the crochet hook from the front-to-back, to facade, around the following double crochet, YO the crochet hook and draw up one loop, YO the crochet hook and drag through two of the loops on crochet hook * replicate from *to* four more times; YO the crochet hook and pull through all six residual loops on crochet hook

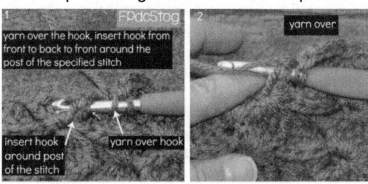

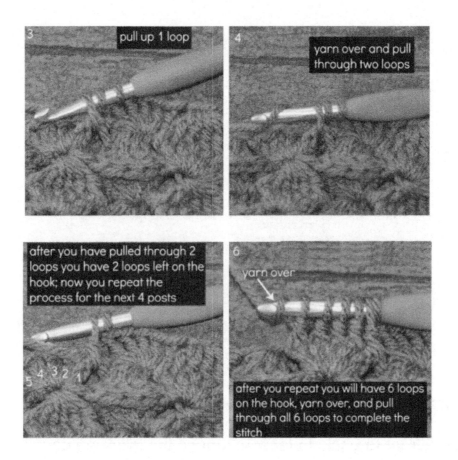

Chain 25

Row 1 (RS): 2 double crochet in the 4th ch from the hook (Note: the skipped three chains count as one double crochet st), double crochet5tog, ch 1, * skip the subsequent ch, five double crochet in the subsequent chain, double crochet5tog, ch 1 *. Replicate from * to * to the last two chains; skip the subsequent ch, three double crochet in the last chain.

Row 2: chain 3 (Note: the chain three taken as one double crochet stitch), flip; Front-post-double crochet2tog, work five double crochet in the subsequent ch, * skip the subsequent reduction, work Front-post-double crochet5tog, chain 1, work five double crochet in the subsequent ch *. Replicate from * to * crossways to the last four stitches. Skip the subsequent decrease; Front-post-double crochet2tog then work one double crochet in the last double crochet of the row

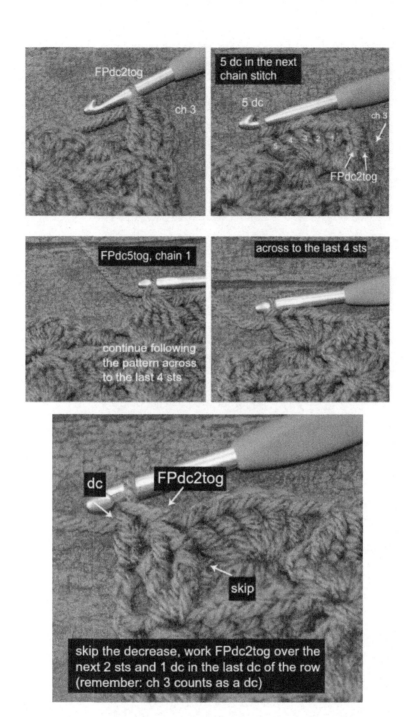

Row 3: chain 3 (Note: the chain three taken as one double crochet stitch), flip; 2 double crochet in the subsequent decrease, work Front-post-double crochet5tog, ch 1, * work five double crochet in the subsequent ch, skip the subsequent decrease, work Front-post-double crochet5tog, ch 1 *. Replicate from * to * crossways to the last two stitches. Work 2 double crochet in the subsequent decrease and one double crochet in the last double crochet.

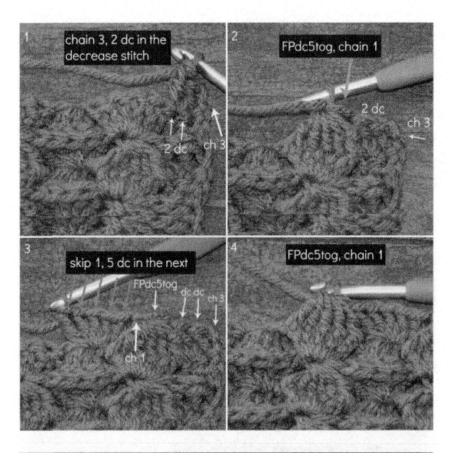

1. chain 3, 2 dc in the decrease stitch
   2 dc ch 3

2. FPdc5tog, chain 1
   2 dc ch 3

3. skip 1, 5 dc in the next
   FPdc5tog dc dc ch 3
   ch 1

4. FPdc5tog, chain 1

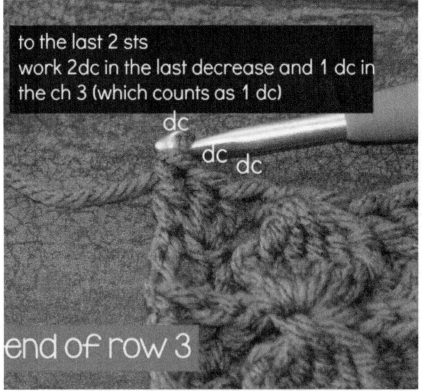

to the last 2 sts
work 2dc in the last decrease and 1 dc in the ch 3 (which counts as 1 dc)

dc
dc dc

end of row 3

Replicate Row 2 and Row 3: four times

Replicate Row 2 1 more time

There is no need to finish it off and proceed to the border.

Border

Row 1: chain 2, flip, 1 half-double-crochet in the following st, 1 single crochet in every of the following 5 stitches, skip the ch1, 1 half-double-crochet in the following st, 1 single crochet in every of the following 5 stitches, skip the ch st, 1 half-double-crochet in the following st, 1 single crochet in every of the following 5 stitches, 1 half-double-crochet in the last st, (19)ch 1 flip to complete the work along the side corner

R2: half-double-crochet 19 times equally along the side corner, chain 1, flip to finish the work along the initial chain row

R3: single crochet 19 times equally along the bottom corner, chain 1, flip to finish the work along the side corner

R4: half-double-crochet 19 times equally along the side corner, chain 1, flip to finish the work along the 1st row of the border

You are now back to the initial corner, two single crochet in every chain stitch (corner), flip one FPdc in every st crossway, two single crochet in every ch st (corner), flip to complete the work along the side corner

one FPdc in every st crossway, two single crochet in every chain stitch (corner), flip to finish the work along the initial chain row

one FPdc in every st crossway, two single crochet in every chain stitch (corner), flip to finish the work along the final corner

one FPdc in every st crossway, finish off with an invisible join and weave in ends.

Stitch 05: Cable Stitch

This stitch looks similar to one twisted rope and you can use it in decoration projects. It is good to make borders of hats, sweaters and scarves. Follow these directions to make cable stitches:

If you want to make one crocheted cable, you should have four stitches on your crochet hook. For this purpose, you have to chain in multiples of four and add three. For instance, four cables can be 16 stitches + 3 will be equal to 19. Hence, the 19 chain stitches will be there. Now, single crochet (SC) in the second stitch from the crochet hook and in every stitch of this chain.

Now chain three and flip.

Avoid the subsequent stitch, dc (double crochet) in every of the subsequent three stitches.

Now, insert the crochet hook, from front-to-back, into the initial stitch avoided.

Pull up one loop, sloppily (loosely), bring this loop toward top of your final double crochet (dc) worked, and complete this double crochet with one yarn over (YO), and over the loops.

Replicate 3,4&5 steps crossways the row. Finish this row with one double crochet in the final stitch.

Chain (ch) 1 and flip, sc (single crochet) in every stitch crossways the row.

Replicate the steps by starting from 2nd step.

In the photo, you can see the three cable stitch rows and these are completed.

Chapter 3 – Learn how to make Popcorn Stitch, Seed Stitch and Shell Stitch

There are three modern stitches that prove helpful to increase the beauty and versatility of your designs:

Stitch 06: Popcorn Stitch

You can easily make popcorn stitch by following all the directions properly. You have to make clusters with double crochet in similar stitch. You can follow the given tutorial to make your work easy:

1. Make one foundation chain that you can easily divide by 3. SC in the second stitch from the crochet hook and in every crochet stitch of this chain.

2. Ch (chain) 1 and flip, SC in the subsequent 2 stitches. * In the subsequent stitch, make 5 DC, keeping the final loop of every stitch on the crochet hook.

3. Sl St (slip stitch) into complete six loops on your crochet hook.

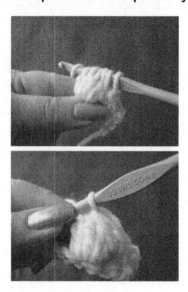

4. SC in the subsequent 3 stitches.

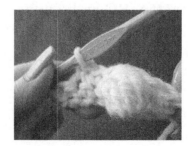

5. Replicate 2,3,and4 crosswise the row, start at * in the 2nd step.

6. Chain (CH) 1 and flip, SC in every stitch crosswise the row. (In your popcorn stitch, SC in the middle stitch.)

(SC (SC) in the middle stitch of back area of your popcorn stitch.)

Replicate the series of steps, such as 2,3,4and5, to make desired number of rows to complete this project.

(Two complete rows of popcorn stitch.)

(Three complete rows of popcorn stitch.)

2nd Tutorial for Popcorn Stitch

The popcorn crochet looks really nice because the round and compact oval stitches will give a unique look to your fabric. It may take a bit more time or efforts, but it will be fun to work in the front and back of the fabric. You need to work 5 double-crochet popcorn stitches that may pop to the front design:

Start 5 double crochet stitches in the similar stitch and drop the loop from your hook.

Pop in your hook from front to back under the upper two loops of the initial dual crochet of the group.

Grasp the plummeted loop with your hook and drag it through your stitch.

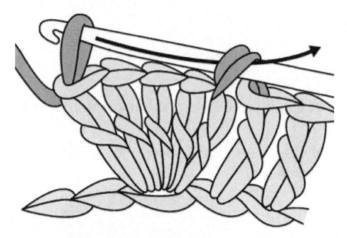

You can notice complete front-popping popcorn.

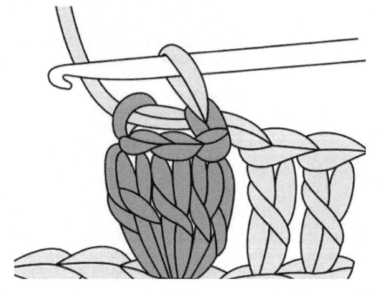

Now it is time to work on the back of the pattern:

Work the 5 dc stitches in the similar stitch. Drop the ring from your hook and pop in your hook from back to front under the upper 2 loops of the initial dc of the group. Grasp the dropped circle with your hook and pull it over the stitch.

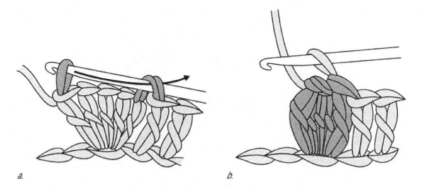

You can see complete back-popping popcorn.

Stitch 07: Shell Stitch

Shell stitch is really beautiful because you can use this stitch in any pattern as per your wish. You can use it to make border or create a variety of patterns, such as beanie, scarf, shrug, etc. See the given tutorial:

This stitch is really simple, just follow the pattern and you are done.

Initiate with one chain.

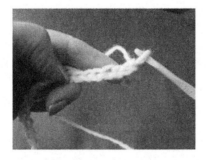

Now double crochet (dc) in the third stitch from your crochet hook.

You will make four more dc (double crochet) stitches in the similar stitch.

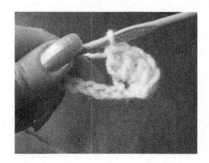

Omit the subsequent three stitches, and make five double crochet in the subsequent stitch.

Replicate 4th step crosswise the row.

Now, at the finishing point of this row, flip and sl st (slip stitch) in the initial three stitches, now chain 2, form four double crochet (dc) in the similar stitch. Replicate 4th crosswise the row. Replicate 6th step for every next row of your shell stitch.

Stitch 08: Seed Stitch

There are only seven steps that will help you to learn this stitch. This stitch will be easy to work with the alternate working of double and single crochet. This stitch looks like a close stitch and you can accomplish it successfully with the help of given tutorial:

1. Initiate with one chain. Flip, SC (single crochet) in the second stitch from your crochet hook.

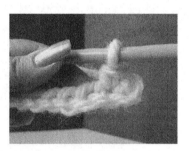

2. DC (double crochet) in the subsequent stitch.

3. SC in the subsequent stitch.

4. Replicated 2nd and 3rd steps crosswise the row.

5. Now you have one complete row of this seed stitch. You can replicate rounds to make this row longer.

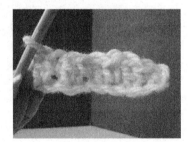

6. At the finishing point of this row, flip. If you are ending in one DC, then you have to SC in the initial stitch. To end in one single crochet, Sl St (slip stitch) in your initial stitch, then chain 2, (it will replace the initial double crochet), SC (single crochet) in the subsequent stitch.

7. You can continue crosswise this row, interchanging it by creating one single crochet (SC) in the DC (double crochet) of the earlier row, and vice-versa. See the photo.

You can replicate this tutorial to make your own patterns with the help of these stitches.

Chapter 4 – Tips to hold the yarn and hook while crocheting?

• There are a number of projects that you can follow because every project is based on the basic crochet stitches from a single stitch to double crochet. In the first step, you need to learn how to hold the yarn and hook:

• There is no critical rule or a specific way to hold the hook and yarn. You can select any way you are comfortable with. For some people, pencil grip is excellent and they hold the hook in the right hand just like a pencil.

• It is necessary to maintain the slight tension in yarn for easy stitching and it will be good to wrap the around your fingers of the other hand opposite to the one you are holding the hook. You can try a way in which you are comfortable to work.

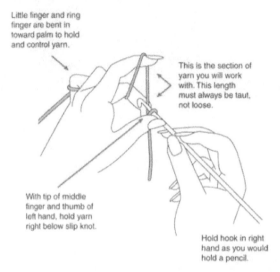

Little finger and ring finger are bent in toward palm to hold and control yarn.

This is the section of yarn you will work with. This length must always be taut, not loose.

With tip of middle finger and thumb of left hand, hold yarn right below slip knot.

Hold hook in right hand as you would hold a pencil.

• In the left hand, you will handle the crochet work and tension of the yarn. The middle finger of the left hand, you can control the yarn, and the index finger and thumb will hold your crochet work.

• In short, there is no strict rule to follow to hold and control the yarn and hook. You can choose any way that helps you to design any pattern comfortably. Some people like pencil grip and they hold it in the right hand just like a pencil.

• Some people prefer knife grip and they also carry the hook just like a knife in the right hand as they hold it while cutting the vegetables.

• For some people. It is more comfortable to control the yarn with the index finger and hold the crochet work with their thumb and middle finger.

You can try any way that can make you comfortable while working.

Chapter 5 – Work on Some Basic Stitches

There is a range of visual effects that you can achieve with the use of right pattern. The crochet looks really cool with the combination of right stitches. You need to tackle the pattern with the use of basic stitches, such as chain stitch, single crochet, and double crochet. Start your practice with basic stitches and then move to advanced stitches. Following are some basic stitches for your help:

Chain Stitch

Every crochet project starts with a chain stitch, and it is important for you to learn this pattern. You can try it with the help of the given below steps:

- In the first step, you will tie a slip loop and glide it over the hook as the first knot.

- Now wrap the yarn around the hook from flipside to frontage and create another loop of yarn on the hook.

- Depict that loop via an already available knot on your hook and complete the chain stitch. Continue this process and design a desired pattern.

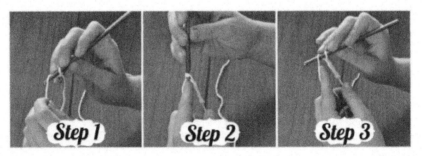

Slip Stitch

If you want something different, then try the pattern of slip stitch. Following are some simple steps for this:

- Make a loop with yarn by wrapping it around your first two fingers.

- The hook should be inserted into the first loop of the yard and try to reach for one loop from behind.

- Hook will help you to grab the yarn at the back of the loop and pull it all the way through.

• Pull to make your slip knot tight and the following picture will help you to tie this knot. You will get one loop and dual pieces of yarn. Carefully cut the free end and another will be known as working end. This will be used to crochet.

Single Crochet

Single crochet is really simple and the following steps will make your work easy:

• Insert your hook into the 2nd chain from hook and pass the yarn under both loops to make a V-shaped chain at the top of the stitch.

• Yarn over and draw a new loop via existing stitch and now you will get two loops on your hook.

• It is time to yarn over once again.

• Draw the loop back and on the hook and continue this process.

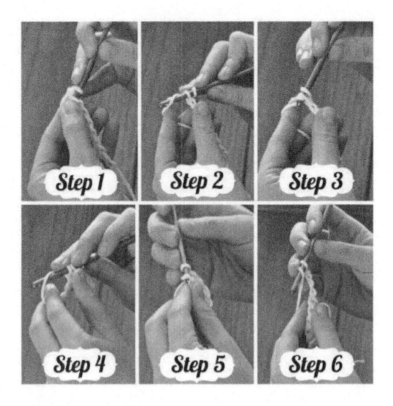

Double Crochet

This crochet is three times taller than a single crochet stitch. You can complete it at a faster rate and to do it, you have to create a double loop at the first stage.

- Yarn over and put on the hook into 2nd stitch.

- Yarn over once again and then draw the yarn with the help of a loop.

- You should have three loops on the hook and yarn over to draw the first two loops on your hook.

- Now your hook will have two loops and you can draw two more loops over your hook. Continue the DC after previous SC row.

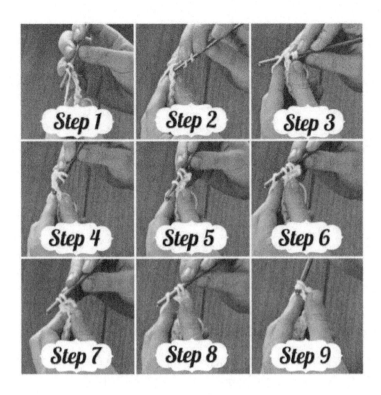

Half Double Crochet

It is a unique design with some glimpses of single crochet and double crochet on the basis of its height.

- It can be completed through particular steps used on the double crochet.

- Just yarn over, insert your hook in the stitch that you are working on and draw the loop back via existing stitch.

- Your hook should have three loops and to complete the stitch, you need to yarn over and draw a new knot back through all existing knots on the hook.

- The following image will give you a better idea of half double crochet:

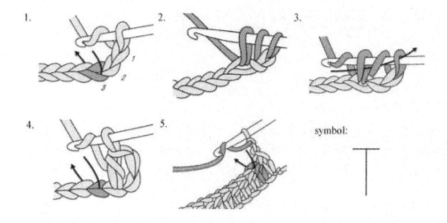

symbol:

Tips to Make an FPdc

It is a specialized version of double crochet via front post. The actual process is same, but the only thing is the insertion of loops on the hook.

- Start by yarning over and then run the hook from right to the left direction or in the vertical position of the stitches.

- Yarn over once again and then pull it back after the post. It will help you to create a third loop on the hook.

- Now it is time to follow the similar process just like you follow while designing double crochet design.

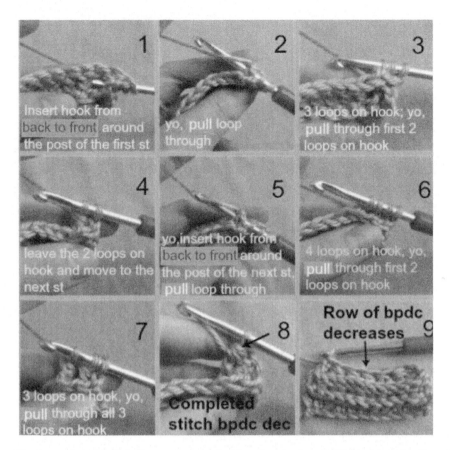

1. Insert hook from back to front around the post of the first st

2. yo, pull loop through

3. 3 loops on hook; yo, pull through first 2 loops on hook

4. leave the 2 loops on hook and move to the next st

5. yo, insert hook from back to front around the post of the next st, pull loop through

6. 4 loops on hook, yo, pull through first 2 loops on hook

7. 3 loops on hook, yo, pull through all 3 loops on hook

8. Completed stitch bpdc dec

9. Row of bpdc decreases

If you want to learn crochet, then in initial level, it will be good to try these patterns. These will help you to become a master in your work.

Conclusion

There are different types of stitches in Crochet, but in the beginning, you can focus on small stitches like a chain. You will make an oval symbol by pulling this loop through another loop to make an interlocking oval. The single crochet is known as a squat cross that is slightly smaller in the length than double crochet. The symbol of double crochet contains a bar in the middle of its post. Remaining symbols are arranged in the line with the same reasoning. The symbol of the short stitch will be short as well, but the puffs out stitches may have similar symbols.

African Flower Crochet

Learn to Crochet Basic African Flower Hexagon And Use It In Wonderful Crochet Projects

Introduction

You browse Pinterest, looking for new inspiration. You want to make something that is new and exciting, and you are tired of the same old stitches. But, you are also short on time, and you don't want to have to spend hours trying to learn a new stitch.

You want something that's easy to make, something you can do in a single afternoon, and something that gives you the results you want. You want to learn a stitch like the African Hexagon stitch.

But when you look at the photos of the stitch, it feels overwhelming. You want to make something that looks like that, but it seems impossible. How do you get the shape of a flower in the center of the stitch, but yet you have a hexagon around the border?

It looks difficult, and like something that's going to take a lot of time for you to learn how to do.

I would love to be able to make the hexagon stitch, but it looks so difficult.

I want to make the African Hexagon stitch, but with all the different shapes and colors, I don't know if I can.

I want to make the hexagon stitch, but how am I supposed to make the edges a hexagon and a flower in the center?

If you haven't ever made this stitch before, you are sure to feel confused. But, I am here to clear this up for you. Using an easy, step by step method that anyone can understand, I am going to show you how to make the African flower stitch in mere hours.

Sit down and grab your crochet hook, your favorite yarn, and brew a cup of coffee – you are about to learn how to make the African flower you have wanted. It's so much easier than you think it is, and with the right set of directions, anyone can learn how to do it.

Let me show you a stitch that is going to open the door to a whole new world of crochet. It might look hard now, but the projects you can make are incredible, and you will be so very glad you did.

Chapter 1 – Creating The African Flower Hexagon Stitch

With all the different stitches you can make with crochet, it can be hard to find something new. The African Hexagon flower stitch, you can get a fresh, new look without having to stress about the stitch.

Though this is considered a single unit, much like a granny square, you are going to create it using a combination of single and double crochet. Don't worry, for as intimidating as it looks, you'll find that it's both fast and incredibly easy to make if you have the right set of directions.

Before we get into those directions, however, you need to gather all your supplies. None of these flowers take much yarn, and you can easily use your scraps to assemble them. However, if you want to use fresh yarn to make them, use a skein in each color you choose.

You will need a size G crochet hook, and for many of the projects you use these flowers to create, you will also need a yarn needle to sew them together. A yarn needle is not necessary for making the flowers themselves, however, so don't worry about that at this point.

Keep your stitches even throughout, and change colors as you like. As I said, these are a great way to use up scraps, but you can do it however you want.

Once you have all your supplies, you are ready to get started.

Let's start your flower.

To begin, chain 5. Make a slip stitch into the first stitch, forming a ring.

Next, chain 3. You are going to count this chain 3 as your first double crochet stitch. Work 1 double crochet stitch into the center of this ring you have just created. Chain 1, then work 2 more double crochet stitches into the center of the ring.

As I said, the first chain 3 you have made counts as your first double crochet, so at this point you should now have a set of 4 double crochet stitches separated by a chain space.

Chain 1, and double crochet in the center of the ring 2 times, chain 1 again, then double crochet in the center of the ring 2 more times. Chain 1, and double crochet in the center of the ring 2 times, chain 1 again, then double crochet in the center of the ring 2 more times. Chain 1, and double crochet in the center of the ring 2 times, chain 1 again, then double crochet in the center of the ring 2 more times.

Continue to work with this same sequence until you have a total of 6 groups in the center of the ring. These will be groups of 2 double crochet, chain space, followed by 2 double crochet.

By this time you should be back to the beginning, with your final stitch next to your chain 3 that you made at first. Join with a slip stitch to the top stitch in this chain 3, closing your loop and forming a complete disc.

Tie off this color, and join with a new color of your choice.

Now it's time to add the next row to the center of the flower.

To join the next color to the flower, insert the hook into the chain space, and grab the yarn. Pull it through, then push the hook through the chain space once more. Bring the yarn up and around the hook, then grab the yarn and pull it through.

You have made a single crochet stitch.

Chain 3.

Next, you are going to make 1 double crochet stitch into this same space you just pulled the yarn through.

Chain 1. Now, work 2 more double crochet stitches in the same space as you made your first double crochet stitch. The space is going to be stretched to accommodate the amount of stitches are putting into it, but don't worry about that, it will be fixed as you move along the row.

Chain 1, and work 2 double crochet into the next space.

Make 2 double crochet stitches into the next space, then chain 1, then make 2 double crochet into the next chain space. Make 2 double crochet stitches into the next space, then chain 1, then make 2 double crochet into the next chain space.

Make 2 double crochet stitches into the next space, then chain 1, then make 2 double crochet into the next chain space. Make 2 double crochet stitches into the next space, then chain 1, then make 2 double crochet into the next chain space.

Make 2 double crochet stitches into the next space, then chain 1, then make 2 double crochet into the next chain space. Make 2 double crochet stitches into the next space, then chain 1, then make 2 double crochet into the next chain space.

Make 2 double crochet stitches into the next space, then chain 1, then make 2 double crochet into the next chain space. Make 2 double crochet stitches into the next space, then chain 1, then make 2 double crochet into the next chain space.

It's important that you keep track of where you are on the pattern, but this is easy to do when you are watching your stitches as you work.

Join with a slip stitch when you get back to the beginning. By now you should have 6 groups of 2 double crochet, chain space, 2 double crochet, 2 double crochet, chain space, 2 double crochet.

Now you have finished the end of the second row, and you can see the center shape of your flower formed.

Now add the petals to the center of your flower.

Begin the next row the same as you have the previous rows, with a chain 3. This is the first double crochet on the row, and will be counted with the rest of the double crochets as you work.

As this is the petal of the flower, you are going to work enough double crochet stitches in the space to form a rounded edge. To do this, work 6 more double crochet stitches in the same stitch as you have made your chain 3 space.

Count to make sure you have the right number of double crochet stitches. You are going to have a total of 7 double crochet stitches in a single chain space, as the first chain 3 you made counts as the first double crochet stitch on the row.

Next, bring the yarn up and over the hook, then make another double crochet in the next chain space.

Work 6 more double crochet stitches in the same stitch as you have made your chain 3 space.

Count to make sure you have the right number of double crochet stitches. You are going to have a total of 7 double crochet stitches in a single chain space.

Next, bring the yarn up and over the hook, then make another double crochet in the next chain space.

Work 6 more double crochet stitches in the same stitch as you have made your chain 3 space.

Count to make sure you have the right number of double crochet stitches. You are going to have a total of 7 double crochet stitches in a single chain space.

Next, bring the yarn up and over the hook, then make another double crochet in the next chain space.

Work 6 more double crochet stitches in the same stitch as you have made your chain 3 space.

Count to make sure you have the right number of double crochet stitches. You are going to have a total of 7 double crochet stitches in a single chain space.

Next, bring the yarn up and over the hook, then make another double crochet in the next chain space.

Work 6 more double crochet stitches in the same stitch as you have made your chain 3 space.

Count to make sure you have the right number of double crochet stitches. You are going to have a total of 7 double crochet stitches in a single chain space.

Next, bring the yarn up and over the hook, then make another double crochet in the next chain space.

Work 6 more double crochet stitches in the same stitch as you have made your chain 3 space.

Count to make sure you have the right number of double crochet stitches. You are going to have a total of 7 double crochet stitches in a single chain space.

Next, bring the yarn up and over the hook, then make another double crochet in the next chain space.

With each rounded edge you make, you can see the shape of the flower coming together. Continue until you have reached the beginning of the flower.

Now it's time to shape the hexagon out of the flower shape.

Join the yarn with a slip stitch, finishing the row.

Cut this color, then join the next color to the flower. Remember to push the hook through the space, then bring the yarn up and over the side of the hook. Yarn pull the yarn through the space, then finish forming your single crochet stitch, attaching the yarn to the flower.

This is going to count as the first single crochet stitch on the loop. Next, follow the edge of the flower as you work 6 more single crochet stitches along the side of the petal.

Counting the first stitch you made, you now have a total of 7 single crochet stitches on the flower.

In the next stitch, you will form a double crochet. make sure the yarn reaches down to the space in the row below, you can see in the photo where this ought to be. This is going to be a very tall stitch, but it forms the shape of the flower.

Once this double crochet stitch is completed, form 7 more single crochet stitches in the next 7 stitches on the flower.

In the next stitch, you will form a double crochet. make sure the yarn reaches down to the space in the row below, you can see in the photo where this ought to be. This is going to be a very tall stitch, but it forms the shape of the flower.

Once this double crochet stitch is completed, form 7 more single crochet stitches in the next 7 stitches on the flower.

In the next stitch, you will form a double crochet. make sure the yarn reaches down to the space in the row below, you can see in the photo where this ought to be. This is going to be a very tall stitch, but it forms the shape of the flower.

Once this double crochet stitch is completed, form 7 more single crochet stitches in the next 7 stitches on the flower.

In the next stitch, you will form a double crochet. make sure the yarn reaches down to the space in the row below, you can see in the photo where this ought to be. This is going to be a very tall stitch, but it forms the shape of the flower.

Once this double crochet stitch is completed, form 7 more single crochet stitches in the next 7 stitches on the flower.

In the next stitch, you will form a double crochet. make sure the yarn reaches down to the space in the row below, you can see in the photo where this ought to be. This is going to be a very tall stitch, but it forms the shape of the flower.

Once this double crochet stitch is completed, form 7 more single crochet stitches in the next 7 stitches on the flower.

In the next stitch, you will form a double crochet. make sure the yarn reaches down to the space in the row below, you can see in the photo where this ought to be. This is going to be a very tall stitch, but it forms the shape of the flower.

Once this double crochet stitch is completed, form 7 more single crochet stitches in the next 7 stitches on the flower.

You should now be back to the beginning of your flower. Remember to join with a slip stitch at the end of the row, sealing the ring of the flower.

The Final Two Rows

Cut the yarn, then join with a new color. Remember to push the hook through the yarn space, then yarn over from the other side. Grab the yarn with your hook, then draw it through the chain space. Form the rest of the single crochet stitch.

You are going to chain 3 with this new color, and count it as the first double crochet stitch on the row.

Double crochet into the next stich on the row, then double crochet into the stitch after that. Double crochet into the next stich on the row, then double crochet into the stitch after that. Continue to work your way up the side of the flower, making only 1 stitch in each of the stitches along the way.

You should now be at the center of the first petal on the flower. This is when you are going to form the angle of the hexagon. To do this, double crochet in this stitch, chain 1, then double crochet into this same stitch once more. Double crochet in the next stitch, double crochet in the next stitch, and double crochet into the next stitch. You are going to continue with this set of double crochet, one in each stitch until you reach the center of the next petal.

Now, chain 1, then double crochet into this same stitch once more. Double crochet in the next stitch, double crochet in the next stitch, and double crochet into the next stitch. You are going to continue with this set of double crochet, one in each stitch until you reach the center of the next petal.

Next, chain 1, then double crochet into this same stitch once more. Double crochet in the next stitch, double crochet in the next stitch, and double crochet into the next stitch. You are going to continue with this set of double crochet, one in each stitch until you reach the center of the next petal.

Again, chain 1, then double crochet into this same stitch once more. Double crochet in the next stitch, double crochet in the next stitch, and double crochet into the next stitch. You are going to continue with this set of double crochet, one in each stitch until you reach the center of the next petal.

Again, chain 1, then double crochet into this same stitch once more. Double crochet in the next stitch, double crochet in the next stitch, and double crochet into the next stitch. You are going to continue with this set of double crochet, one in each stitch until you reach the center of the next petal.

One more time, chain 1, then double crochet into this same stitch once more. Double crochet in the next stitch, double crochet in the next stitch, and double crochet into the next stitch. You are going to continue with this set of double crochet, one in each stitch until you reach the center of the next petal.

Join with a slip stitch, then cut the yarn. You are going to work 1 more row in a new color.

Cut the yarn, then join with a new color. Remember to push the hook through the yarn space, then yarn over from the other side. Grab the yarn with your hook, then draw it through the chain space. Form the rest of the single crochet stitch.

You are going to chain 3 with this new color, and count it as the first double crochet stitch on the row.

Double crochet into the next stich on the row, then double crochet into the stitch after that. Double crochet into the next stich on the row, then double crochet into the stitch after that. Continue to work your way up the side of the flower, making only 1 stitch in each of the stitches along the way.

You should now be at the center of the first petal on the flower. This is when you are going to form the angle of the hexagon. To do this, double crochet in this stitch, chain 1, then double crochet into this same stitch once more. Double crochet in the next stitch, double crochet in the next stitch, and double crochet into the next stitch. You are going to continue with this set of double crochet, one in each stitch until you reach the center of the next petal.

Now, chain 1, then double crochet into this same stitch once more. Double crochet in the next stitch, double crochet in the next stitch, and double crochet into the next stitch. You are going to continue with this set of double crochet, one in each stitch until you reach the center of the next petal.

Next, chain 1, then double crochet into this same stitch once more. Double crochet in the next stitch, double crochet in the next stitch, and double crochet into the next stitch. You are going to continue with this set of double crochet, one in each stitch until you reach the center of the next petal.

Again, chain 1, then double crochet into this same stitch once more. Double crochet in the next stitch, double crochet in the next stitch, and double crochet into the next stitch. You are going to continue with this set of double crochet, one in each stitch until you reach the center of the next petal.

Again, chain 1, then double crochet into this same stitch once more. Double crochet in the next stitch, double crochet in the next stitch, and double crochet into the next stitch. You are going to continue with this set of double crochet, one in each stitch until you reach the center of the next petal.

One more time, chain 1, then double crochet into this same stitch once more. Double crochet in the next stitch, double crochet in the next stitch, and double crochet into the next stitch. You are going to continue with this set of double crochet, one in each stitch until you reach the center of the next petal.

Join with a slip stitch.

Tie off, and that's it! You have completed your first African Hexagon Stitch.

You can clearly see all the different rows and the longer stitches in the photo, as well as how I finished the hexagon. Remember to take your time with this, and count as you go.

This is a very straight forward pattern, and when you follow each of the steps you are going to see the shape come together right before your very eyes. Remember that practice makes perfect, and the more you practice these hexagons, the easier they will be to complete.

Tie off each one as you finish it, then set it aside. When you have enough, you can make virtually any project you can think of!

Chapter 2 – African Flower Hexagon Projects

All About that Flower Baby Blanket

Photo made by: pandatomic

Use scrap yarn or 1 skein of yarn for each of the colors you wish to have in your project. Use a size G crochet hook, and a yarn needle.

For this blanket, you can make as many hexagons as you like. To make it the same size I did, you will need a total of 106. I did row by row of 10, 9, 10.

You are going to start this project by making each of the hexagon stitches as I outlined in the last chapter. Remember to keep your stitches even so each of the flowers turn out close to the same size.

As you can see by the photo, I used white as the primary color, with red and blue as the secondary and third colors. You can follow the same color scheme as I used, or you can choose your own. If you use scrap yarn, you are going to end up with an entirely hodge podge blanket.

Remember to keep the stitches even so all the flowers end up close to the same size, and as you complete each one check it against the others you have made to ensure that it's the right size. Tie off each one as you finish it, then set it aside until you have completed all the flowers.

The first strip has 10 flowers in it, then the next strip has 9 flower in it. The next strip has 10 flowers in it, then the next strip has 9 flower in it. Follow this pattern until you run out of the flowers, then tie off.

Now, you are going to finish the blanket with a border. Join the color of your choice to the side of the blanket with a slip stitch, then work a single crochet row around the entire blanket. You can add another row if you like, or tie it off as it is now.

That's it! Your African baby blanket is done and ready for that special little one in your life.

An African Hexagon Pin Cushion

Photo made by: Charyl

Use scrap yarn or 1 skein of yarn for each of the colors you wish to have in your project. Use a size G crochet hook, and a yarn needle.

You will also need stuffing for the center of the piece.

This is a little project, and you can likely make it in just a single afternoon if you try. Decide which color scheme you want, or use the scrap yarn you have in your basket to put together a pin cushion of scraps. Either way, you are going to end up with an adorable project you can use for all your other crafting needs.

If you would rather not use your scrap yarn, you can purchase each of the colors you need for your own particular scheme.

Once you have chosen the color scheme that works for you, you are ready to form the flowers. Follow the same sequence that I outlined in chapter 1. Take your time, and make both the flowers as close to the same size as you can. Of course, following the same pattern you are going to end up with flowers that are close to the same size anyway, but if you make the stitches the same tension, you will get an even better fit.

Make one, then repeat for the other end of the pin cushion.

Once you have both of your flowers created and set aside, you are going to make the center strip.

Start by measuring around the outside of both your flowers, and chain a length that is equal to this measurement. Single crochet across the row. Chain 1, turn, and single crochet back to the other side. chain 1, turn, and single crochet back to the beginning.

Chain 1, turn, and single crochet to the other side.

You can make this strip as thin or as thick as you like. When you are happy with how thick it is, tie it off.

Take your yarn needle now, and fit the strip to one of the flowers as you sew it together. Sew all the way around the flower, using one part of the flower against the edge of the strip as you work.

Work your way around the entire border, and you will finish with a cup shape.

Next, sew the opposite flower to the top of the piece, only this time, leave one of the ends open, so you can stuff the pin cushion with your stuffing.

Stuff the center of the flower firmly, making sure all ends are tucked in. Stuff as firmly as you like, the firmer the better, in my opinion! When you are happy with the size of the flower, tie it off.

Snip off the loose ends, and your pin cushion is ready for action!

Conclusion

There you have it, everything you need to know to make your own African flower stitch, and what you need to know to put it into as many projects as you like. I hope this book gave you the inspiration you need to make the African Hexagon, and to put it into the projects you have been wanting to make.

With the two projects provided in this book, you are going to realize just how easy it is to bring this stitch into your day to day crochet. Think of it as a spin on the granny square, and a way you can show off your skills in a whole new way.

You don't have to be an expert at crochet, and with practice, you are going to see that it's just as easy as single and double. All you need to do is keep track of where you are on the hexagon and the flower, and where you need to put the chain spaces.

It's going to take some deliberate effort for a while, but witch practice, it's all going to come as second nature, and you'll be able to form the flowers without giving it a second thought.

Have fun and express yourself with all the different colors you can use, and make the flowers as large as you want with a few extra rows on the border. There's no end to the ways you can make your own African Hexagon flowers, and when you let your creativity flow, you can make them even more elaborate.

The African Hexagon stitch may look hard, but you will quickly see that you can make it no matter what your skill level happens to be, and the projects you can make are going to impress anyone and everyone who sees them.

Now get out there and show the world what you can do.

Happy crocheting.

One Day Afghan Crochet
10 Pretty Afghan Crochet Patterns You Can Master in One Day!

Introduction

Crochet is a beautiful and unique form of domestic art. In countries in the east, domestic skills and arts like these are very popular and are very values. As difficult as it looks, it is worth learning due to its uniqueness and value as well as beauty. Crochet items have become really popular in the recent past. All these age old fashions that are ever green and golden classics are making thrilling comebacks and crochet is one of those trends. This will never get old. A crochet throw blanket on your couch or accent chair or a crochet article of clothing will always something to value in the winter months.

As beautiful and colorful as crochet is, its items that are pleasing to the eyes are often very heavy and unpleasing on the pocket. Crochet can be expensive. Well with this book that will not be the case anymore. We will show you how to make beautifully ethnic as well as unusual items of clothing and d é cor in no time. With the simple and easy to follow steps, you will be able to complete these projects in a single day. Being able to make your own items from crochet has myriad benefits. Not only are you able to add your sense of personal touch but they are also ridiculously customizable. You can go for whatever colors and patterns that you like and make things that match perfectly with your personality and with the vibe and d é cor of your house. How exciting is that? So without further delay, lets grab those crochet hooks and get crocheting.

Chapter 1 – Cozy Afghan Blankets

Anybody who is new to the amazing and colorful world of arts and crafts would most certainly be intimidated by something that sounds as complicated as crochet stich. While it sounds like a daunting task it is definitely not difficult at all to do. With the easy and simple guidelines, we have discussed in this book you will be able to master it in no time at all.

We will take you through afghan crochet stich patterns of all kinds but first let us look at how to make blankets. Blankets are a beautiful accessory to be added anywhere in your house. It can liven up your boring bed spread or awaken the plain couch in your living room when used as a throw. The touch stich of personal sense that you will get by making your own is just an added bonus. So let us learn a few different kinds of afghan crochet stich patterns for blankets.

Project 01: Rainbow Afghan Blanket

This is a beautiful and colorful blanket that you can use as a throw or curl up into while you read your favorite book.

Materials Required

1. Crochet Needle/Hook – These come in different sizes. The best to start with when you are a beginner is the I-9 hook. Here we will be using a K hook.

2. Yarn (color of your chain choice) – Get solid, bright colored yarn when you are a beginner since multi colored chain stiches will be difficult to distinguish when you are at beginner level. Get worsted weight yarn made out of wool fiber or acrylic fiber.

3. A pair of scissors – Make sure it is a nice and sharp one.

Methods

1. First thing to decide is what do you want the width of your blanket to be. Measure it out and plan accordingly. Planning ahead is very important in crochet stiches especially if you are a beginner to avoid any time waste and effort. Here we will use 122 chain stiches to make medium sized blanket.

2. Once the width is decided, make a classic crochet stich chain stich or chain stich of the desired length. In our example we will uses 121.

3. Now for row 1, using the color of your choice, make a single crochet stich in to the second crochet hook from the initial chain stich and then keep working a single crochet stich in every single chain until the end. When you are making 120 stiches this will have created your foundation row .

4. Now for row 2, keep using the same color as you were using before for the chain stich, chain stich 1 and then and then make a turn. Now make 1 single crochet stich into the next stich, and 1 and then make a turn chain into the next stich. Do this in repetition and finish with a single crochet stich in the last chain stich of the row. You have now created your first row of the chain stiches. These are referred to as bubble or popcorn stiches.

5. Now for row 3, keep using the same color as you were using before for the chain stich, chain stich 3 and then make a turn. Into

the next chain stich work one single crochet stich. (Remember that this single crochet stich is worked into the top of what was a turn chain in the previous row.) Into the next chain stich, make and then make a turn chain stich. (Remember, this and then make a turn chain stich is made into the top of what was a single crochet stich in the previous row.) Now single crochet stich in next chain stich, and then make a turn the chain stich in next chain stich* across. This way you will make and then make a turn chain stich into the last single chain stich of the last row and then a double crochet stich into chain stich was the and then make a turning chain stich in the previous row.

6. For row number 4, repeat the exact same procedure as the previous row 3. Each row starts with a chain stich 3 and ends with a double crochet stich. Between these two, you simply be working with a repeat of single crochet stiches and turn chain stiches. Isn't that easy?

7. Here we have used different color for each chain in a row. The color chain changes of yarn will happen in row 5 and after that in row 7 after which every other row will be a different color. And the resulting pattern is shown as an image below.

Project 02: Afghan Throw

This is ideal for use over your bed or even to decorate a colorful couch. The pattern is very ethnic and afghan and not difficult to do at all. Just the simple steps below.

Material Required

1. Crochet Needle/Hook – These come in different sizes. Here we will be using a H-8 hook.

2. Yarn (color of your chain choice) – Get solid, bright colored yarn when you are a beginner since multi colored chain stiches will be difficult to distinguish when you are at beginner level. Get worsted weight yarn made out of wool fiber or acrylic fiber. Here we will be using three colors, green, white and pink. You can go for any of your choice.

3. A pair of scissors – Make sure it is a nice and sharp one.

Method

1. For row 1, make a chain stich of 143 classic crochet stiches, double crochet stich in 4th chain stich from the hook, and in next chain, chain stich 2, * now skipping 2 chain stich, double crochet in every one of the coming 5 chain chains, stich 2, repeat from and across to the last 5 chain stiches, now skipping 2 chain stiches, double crochet in each stich of last 3 chain stiches and then make a turn.

2. For row 2, chain stich 3, Shell stich in next chain stich 2 space, now skipping 2 make double crochet stich, back post double crochet stich around next double crochet stich, Shell in next chain stich 2 space, repeat from last row across to the last 3 double crochet, skipping 2 double crochet, double crochet in last double crochet and then make a turn.

3. For row 3: Chain stich 3, double crochet in next 2 double crochet, chain stich 2, *skipping 2 double crochet, double crochet in next 2 double crochet, Front post double crochet around next back post double crochet, double crochet in next 2 double crochet, chain stich 2, repeat from * across to the last 5 double crochet, skipping 2 double crochet, double crochet in last 3 double crochet and then make a turn.

4. For row 4: Chain stich 3, Shell in next chain stich 2 space, *skipping 2 double crochet, back post double crochet around next Front post double crochet, Shell stitch in next chain stich 2 space, repeat from * across to the last 3 double crochet, skipping 2 double crochet, double crochet in last double crochet, bind off and then make a turn.

5. For row 5: Join pink in first chain stich, chain stich 2 and then keep going with the 3rd row.

6. For row 6, repeat all the process of row 2.

7. For row 7: repeat all the process of row 3.

8. For row 8: Repeat the process of row 2, bind off and then make a turn.

Chapter 2 – Afghan Booties and Flip Flops

Afghan style f crochet is one of the most beautiful ones. You will never see an afghan crochet article that is not beautiful. It makes everything look so much more ethnic. It adds color to your home.

Another great use of afghan crochet is using it to add color not only to your home and living but also to your wardrobe. A very popular application of afghan crochet is to utilize those beautiful stiches to make flip flops and booties for your young ones as well as for yourself. A lot of people use it for making shawls sweaters and throws but here will discuss the innovative way in which you can make beautiful and colorful flip flops and booties.

Project 03: Afghan Flip Flops Women

These can be the sweetest little accessory to glamorize your feet and at the same time staying comfortable. So let us get started.

Material Required

1. Crochet Needle/Hook – These come in different sizes. Here we will be using a 6mm hook.

1. Yarn (color of your chain choice) – Get solid, bright colored yarn and get worsted weight yarn made out of wool fiber or acrylic fiber. You can go for any of your choice.

2. A pair of scissors

Method

1. Chain 9 stiches. Make 3 single crochet in 2nd chain from the crochet hook, single crochet in next 3 chains, half double crochet in next chain, double crochet in next 2 chains, 7 double crochet in last chain. Now start work across the opposite side and follow this: Double crochet in next 2 chains, half double crochet in next chain, single crochet in next 3 chains. This makes 22 stiches. Remember to stich the marker and shift it up with every single round.

2. 2 single crochet in the next 3 stiches. Single crochet in next 7 stiches. 2 single crochet in next 5 stiches. Single crochet in next 7 stiches. This makes 30 stiches.

3. Single crochet in next stich, 2 single crochet in next stitch. Do this thrice. Single crochet in next 7 stiches. *Single crochet in next stich, 2 single crochet in next stitch and do this 5 times then single crochet in next 7 stiches. This makes 38 stiches. Now just bind off.

4. Count the slip stich, count 7 toward your right side. Here attach another second color of your choosing. Chain 1. Single crochet in same stich. Single crochet 2. Chain 7. Skip 8 stiches, single crochet in next stich. Single crochet 2. Chain 14. Attach with a slip stich with the very first stich of the round

5. Chain 1. Single crochet in same stich. Single crochet. Now attach with slip stich. Bind off.

6. For the strap, begin with a long tail end of 8 inches and this will be a separate piece.

7. Chain 3. Single crochet into 2nd chain from hook. Single crochet 1. Then turn.

8. Chain 1. Single crochet into same stich. Single crochet 1. Now turn.

9. Single crochet in same stich. Tilt 90 degrees. Make 5 single crochet across the side. Single crochet 2 in last stich. Single crochet in the other corner. Bind off after leaving a tail to tie.

The project can also be altered to make adult flip flops or booties, a great idea is to try making the pattern using a flip flop soul as a base and make the shoes wearable outdoors Make them for adults or babies, it will all be easy now.

Chapter 3 – Beautiful Afghan Jewelry

If you are a crocheting fan and a knitting fan, then the afghan crochet is the way to go. Also referred to as "Tunisian" crochet sometimes, afghan crochet is a merger between knitting and crocheting, and the products of these techniques speak for themselves. Whatever you create with the afghan crochet, would have the distinct "knit look" while having been made with a crocheting needle and technique. With this, most people are familiar with the

Afghan blankets, which is a popular manifestation of this crocheting technique. However, much like any other, the technique can be used to make a lot more than just blankets and throws for your living room. The afghan crochet has its own particular stitches and techniques that can be used to make simple crocheted jewelry. For a beginner, this is easy and can be increased in the difficulty level one by one, as each afghan crochet begins with a simple chain stitch, and picks up from there. As always, the crocheting requires a yarn of thread in the choice of your material, and the crocheting hook. However, the afghan crocheting hook is a bit different from the usual one. They are longer than the regular crochet hooks, and have the proper shape on their tip needed to hold the many loops that constitute an afghan crochet. In this guide, we will discuss some easy DIY afghan crochet ideas for fun and stylish jewelry that you can make in an evening and pair with you lovely outfit for a special day.

Project 04: The Tunisian cuff bracelet

Cuff bracelets are an edgy yet elegant jewelry item, and are fairly easy to make with crochet. The Tunisian cuff bracelet is made using afghan crochet technique and gives the unique knitted look. Let's look at a simple technique to make a two colored cuff bracelet.

Materials required

1. Afghan crochet hook, preferably size F.

2. Two colors of yarn thread

3. Scissors, glue etc.

Method

1. Begin with making a slip knot by passing your yarn on the crochet needle. Use the yarn thread to make a loop, and allow the needle to pass through this loop. Around the hook of the needle, wrap the yarn and pull it through the loop.

This will give you a basic slipknot which will serve as a starting point for the chain stitch.

2. Start a simple chain stitch from your slip knot using the first color yarn. This is made simply by wrapping the yarn again on the hook and pulling it through the loop as you did with the slip knot. Do 10 of the chain stitch, more if you want a thicker one, or less stitches if you want a thinner bracelet. This is now the foundation row.

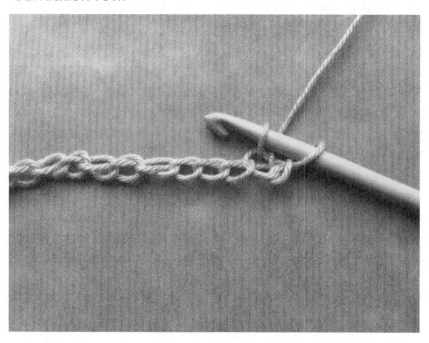

3. With the same color yarn, do the yarn over to make a loop in the second chain stitch and all the following chain stitch loops on the hook.

4. Now use the second color yarn, and use it to yarn over and draw a loop on the first loop that is on your hook. Use the next two loops on the hook to yarn over them a draw another loop. Keep the similar technique for all the next loops until only one is left on your hook. This is your second vertical bar.

5. Continue with the second color yarn, and under the second vertical bar, insert the hook to yarn over and draw a loop. Do the same with inserting hook under the next vertical bar and yarning over to make loops for all the next loops on the hook.

6. Use the first color yarn again to draw a loop by another yarn over the first loop on the hook. Again, use the next two loops on the hook to yarn over them a draw another loop and do it for all the next loops until one loop is left on the hook.

7. Continue with the first color yarn, and under the second vertical bar, insert the hook to yarn over and draw a loop. Do the same with inserting hook under the next vertical bar and yarning over to make loops for all the next loops on the hook.

8. Repeat steps 4 to 7 t increase the length of your cuff bracelet, or keep it at this by finishing off with doing a border of single crochet on around the length of both long sides. On the short side, finish the border 2 single crochets on each stitch in the corner and fasten off.

9. End with making button holes on the edge of one short side, while stitching button on the opposite short side. Your bracelet cuff should look similar to this:

Project 05: Afghan crochet Necklace and earrings

A fairly simple pattern that goes for a long loopy necklace and then for its matching pair of earrings to make a complete set.

Materials

1. Nylon thread yarn of the color of your choice

2. Tapestry needles

3. Afghan hook, crochet hook (size of your choice)

4. Fish hook steel earrings of approximately 1 inch.

Method

Project 6: Necklace: The necklace is made roughly around 20-22 inches.

Row 1. Leave about a space of 10-11 inches' empty on your crochet hook and using the afghan hook, chain stitch 75. Insert the crochet hook on the second stitch, pull a loop through by doing a yarn over, and then insert hook in the next chain stitch, and pull a loop through by doing a yarn over. Finish the first row by doing a work loops off hook. Do this by doing a yarn over by pulling a single loop on the hook. Use the next two loops on the hook to yarn over them a draw another loop. Keep the similar technique for all the next loops until only one is left on your hook.

Row 2. Slipknot the first vertical bar, insert the hook from front to back with the yarn in back. Do a yarn over by pulling a single loop on the hook. Use the next two loops on the hook to yarn over them a draw another loop. Keep the similar technique for all the next loops until only one is left on your hook.

Row 3-5. For these three rows, repeat the technique for row 2.

Button: Use the crochet hook to make a 5 long chain stitch and then from the hook, use the second chain stitch to make 10 single crochet stitches. Fasten off here. Finish the button by making weaving its end through the single crochets for the button hole. Roll the rows of the necklace to a close by sewing the edges of the rows on an angle that causes them to spiral the necklace. Make a 1-inch loop for the other end of the necklace and sew it off, making a button hole.

Project 7: Earing: The earing is made roughly an inch or more for both in the pair.

Row 1. Leave about a space of 8 inches' empty on your crochet hook and using the afghan hook, chain stitch 7. Insert the crochet hook on the second stitch, pull a loop through by doing a yarn over, and then insert hook in all the next chain stitches across, and pull a loop through by doing a yarn over. Finish the first row by doing a work loops off hook. Do this by doing a yarn over by pulling a single loop on the hook. Use the next two loops on the hook to yarn over them a draw another loop. Keep the similar technique for all the next loops until only one is left on your hook.

Row 2 & 3. Do a slip knot from the first vertical bar and insert the hook from front to back with the yarn in back. Do a yarn over by pulling a single loop on the hook. Use the next two loops on the hook to yarn over them a draw another loop. Keep the similar technique for all the next loops until only one is left on your hook. Fasten off after leaving a 12-inch end.

Finish off by threading the ends of the earrings through the fishhooks and do two slip stitches to reinforce them in place with the hooks. Sew the edges at an angle similar to the necklace to give the earrings the same spiral, by sewing the first stitch on the bottom with the second stitch on the top. Your necklace and earrings set will look something like this:

Chapter 4 – Beautiful Afghan Scarves

Afghan scarves are incredibly popular among scar lovers because of their knitted look and use for both warm and cold seasons. Although they require a lot more work than a few simple jewelry items, the techniques of afghan crochet are more or less the same and with slight modifications, can be done by a beginner or an intermediate crocheted. Here we discuss a few patterns to make DIY afghan scarves and make your outfit ensemble a little more edgy and personal.

Project 08: Tunisian crochet scarf

The words afghan crochet and Tunisian crochet often interchange and mean the same thing. A simple overlay of this stitch pattern in the form of a scarf is a great way to go. Opt for a neutral toned warm color to make an equally warm feeling scarf.

Materials

1. A large yarn or about 6-7 skeins of a single colored thread.

2. A 6 mm long afghan crochet hook.

3. Scissors.

Method

Row 1

1. Begin with a slip knot and a foundation row of approximately 42 chain stitches.

2. Start the preparation row by inserting hook into the 2nd chain stitch at the back, yarn over to pull a loop over the hook and continue it on for all the loops across.

3. Use the next two loops on the hook to yarn over them a draw another loop. Keep the similar technique for all the next loops until only one is left on your hook.

4. To make the first forward row, insert hook through the first space as shown in figure right between the vertical strands from right to left and yarn over to pull a loop through, which you leave on the hook. Continue this for all the vertical strands till the very end of the entire row. Leave the last loop. Now insert the hook into the chain stitch and pull a loop onto the hook for all 42 stitches in the chain.

5. Chain a single stitch here, and yarn over to pull a loop through the next two chain stitches, continuing till the end, where you leave one loop on the hook.

Row 2

1. Insert the hook in space next to the first in the figure in between the vertical strands from right to left and yarn over to pull a loop through, which you leave on the hook. Continue this for all the vertical strands till the very end of the entire row and this time include the last loop. Now insert the hook into the chain stitch and pull a loop onto the hook for all 42 stitches in the chain.

2. Chain a single stitch here, and yarn over to pull a loop through the next two chain stitches, continuing till the end, where you leave one loop on the hook.

For rows 3 onwards

Repeat these steps for another 4 rows until the material begins to become of around 70 inches in size and then end with a yarn over to pull a loop through the next two chain stitches, continuing till the end, where you leave one loop on the hook.

Finish off by using the space marked 1 in the first forward row as shown in the figure to pull up a loop and yarn it over to pull further two more loops. Repeat the step by putting hook through the next space and repeat for all the spaces between the vertical strands till the end of row. End with one loop still remaining on the hook. Here, cut the remaining yarn to pull through the remaining loop. Ensuring that the side is facing towards you, make a single crochet along the bind off edge at every stitch. Again, cut the remaining yarn to pull through the remaining loop. For the cast on edge, repeat this pattern. For all the ends, weave in properly and block as you desire for your scarf.

Project 09: Infinity scarf

Material

1. Afghan long hook.

2. Large yarn needle

3. Full yarn of the color and material of your choice

Method

Row 1. To make the first forward row, insert hook through the first space right between the vertical strands from right to left and yarn over to pull a loop through, which you leave on the hook. Chain stitch 17 and use the second loop on the hook to work into pulling up a loop from each stitch in the chain to make 17 loops on the hook. Use the next two loops on the hook to yarn over them a draw another loop. Keep the similar technique for all the next loops until only one is left on your hook.

Row 2. Leave the first stitch and make the second forward row by this time making the hook insert under the back horizontal bar from right to left and yarn over to pull a loop through, which you leave on the hook. Chain stitch 17 and use the second loop on the hook to work into pulling up a loop from each stitch in the chain to make 17 loops on the hook. Use the next two loops on the hook to yarn over them a draw another loop. Keep the similar technique for all the next loops until only one is left on your hook.

Row 3 to onwards. Continue with the steps for Row 2 onwards till the yarn is left enough to stitch up the ends of the scarf. To give the look of the infinity scarf, twist the scarf and stitch the ends together by any seam stitch such as the mattress for a nice and almost invisible seam. You can also opt for keeping the sides straight for the scarf to lack the twisty look, and then sew its ends together. The scarf should come out too look like this:

Infinity scarf is a lot more popular these days, and while both scarves essentially differ in simply sewing together the ends, more or less, it gives you a great room to choose the one you like. You can use a lighter and less warm material yarn to make an open scarf for slightly warmer seasons, whereas an infinity scarf made from warm wool or alpaca that completely covers your neck is a great option for winters. Be sure to know if you are allergic to any of these materials before using them.

Project 10: Isle Cowl

Crochet Hook: 5.5 mm or I/9

Weight of Yarn: (4) Aran and Worsted Weight and Medium Weight (16 to 20 stitches to four inches)

Crochet Gauge: 14 single crochet = 4(ten cm); 16 rounds is equal to four (ten cm) in sc (single crochet) and Isle Chart

Keep an eye on your gauge.

Final Size: 9.5 inches x 22 inches

Material:

- 1 balls of Wheat A
- 1 ball of Sea B
- 1 ball of Grey C
- 1 ball of Seafoam D

Notes: You will work this cowl in rounds and every round worked with RS (right side) face.

The stitches will work in the back loops, unless you work in both loops.

Pick your yarn from old to turn yarns and avoid holes. You can carry colors that are not in use slackly along WS (wrong side) of your work. On subsequent round, you have to work on carried yarn of proceeding round to hide everything.

While changing colors, you will work in the last step of the final stitch of former color with a new color.

COWL Directions:

With A, chain 80 [100], slip st in first chain to form a ring, being careful not to twist chain.

Round 1 (Right Side): Chain 1 (don't consider it as a stitch here and all over), working in both loops, single crochet in similar stitch as join and every chain around, slip stitch in first single crochet to join, 80(100) single crochet.

Round 2: Chain 1, working in the back loops merely and start with 2nd round of Isle Chart, work 20-stitches replicate of Chart in single crochet around.

Working in the back loops merely, work Isle Chart in single crochet until Round 32 is completed, and work in Rounds 1 to 5 again. Tie off.

FINISHING
Now, weave all ends

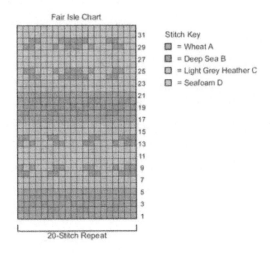

Fair Isle Chart

Stitch Key
☐ = Wheat A
■ = Deep Sea B
☐ = Light Grey Heather C
☐ = Seafoam D

20-Stitch Repeat

Conclusion

For anybody, there is no satisfaction greater than the ability to fashion your own articles of clothing and decor. First of all, the customization that it comes with it is absolutely unmatched. You can alter everything from colors to patterns and designs. about it to cater to your own liking. And as far as making your own stuff goes from crochet goes, it is a phenomenal experience. You can take advantage of this beautiful and fun hobby by practicing the easy beginner friendly projects that you learned from this book. Not only is crocheting fun but it is a great way to pass some time without getting bored. The activities like this that are craft and art related have a very calming effect on your mind. Just put music, get that kettle going and get your grandma on! Hey, we all need that at some point.

These projects are one day and they assure the level of ease assures that you learn afghan style crochet in just one day. How great is that? Make stuff for yourself or impress friends and family, you are a pro!

Most tutorials of the items discussed in the chapters above will make for amazing gifts. Make beautiful ethnic throw blankets to match with your living room d é cor or even to jazz up your plain bedroom. The world is your oyster! Follow the simple, beginner friendly tutorials and you will see is not as difficult as it is made out to be. So without further delay, let us make something colorfully cultural.

Printed in Great Britain
by Amazon

38709942R00057